# The Great Wall of All

Written by Mary Atkinson
Illustrated by Spike Wademan

China

My name is Sying. I live in Beijing, China. Did you know that the Great Wall of China was built hundreds of years ago? There were no motors or electric machines back then. How do you think it was built?

# Contents

The Great Wall      4

The First Wall      6

The Ming Wall      8

Getting Supplies      10

Tools for the Job      12

Lifting Loads      14

Great by Design      16

Gates and Passes      18

Reaching the Top      20

The Great Wall Today      22

Find Out More!      24

Index      24

Look for the **Activity Zone!**
When you see this picture, you will find
an activity to try.

# The Great Wall

The Great Wall of China stretches for 2,150 miles along the northern border of China. It is the longest wall in the world. It was built to keep raiders from the north out of China.

Chinese rulers began to build the wall more than 2,000 years ago. They continued to build and join up parts of the wall until the 1600s. Most of it was built by hand, using very simple tools.

Parts of the Great Wall were built along mountaintops. The steep hills made it hard for raiders to get near the wall.

**raider** a person who enters a place without permission and steals things

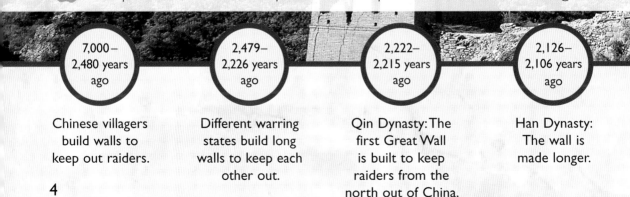

| 7,000– 2,480 years ago | 2,479– 2,226 years ago | 2,222– 2,215 years ago | 2,126– 2,106 years ago |
|---|---|---|---|
| Chinese villagers build walls to keep out raiders. | Different warring states build long walls to keep each other out. | Qin Dynasty: The first Great Wall is built to keep raiders from the north out of China. | Han Dynasty: The wall is made longer. |

4

If the Great Wall were moved to the U.S., it would stretch from New York City to Phoenix, Arizona.

Ming Dynasty Wall (red)

CHINA

This map shows the wall that was built in the Ming Dynasty (1368–1644). It is not in a straight line. Instead, it twists and turns and doubles up on itself.

| 1,424– 1,387 years ago | 1368– 1644 | 1960s and 1970s | Today |
|---|---|---|---|
| Sui Dynasty: Parts of the wall crumble. It is fixed seven times. | Ming Dynasty: The wall is rebuilt and made even longer. | Parts of the wall are pulled down under the communist government. | The wall is being fixed and rebuilt. Scientists are studying it. |

# The First Wall

The first emperor to rule the whole of China was Qin Shi Huangdi (*chin shee hoo-an-dee*). He wanted to stop the people living north of China from raiding Chinese farms. To do this, he ordered that a great wall be built.

Millions of people were forced to work on the wall. In just seven years, they built about 2,500 miles of wall. They worked all summer and winter with little food. Thousands of them died from hunger, disease, or injury.

Frame

Layers of earth and rubble

Parts of the first wall were made of earth and rubble. Workers built a frame and then filled it in. Every four-inch layer was pounded until it was almost as hard as concrete.

emperor   the ruler of an empire, or group of nations

# Ancient Technology

Tower built of brick

Ladder

About 2,300 years ago, people knew how to make some metal tools, such as knives and spades. But most workers could not afford them, so they used sticks, stones, and their hands and feet.

1. Workers probably used stones and wooden poles to pound the earth.

2. They carried dirt and rubble in baskets.

3. Bricks were made of mud. The mud was put in wooden boxes called *molds*. Then the mud was dried in the sun.

The first wall was 25 feet wide at the base and 13 feet wide at the top. It was wide enough for four horses to ride side by side.

# The Ming Wall

Most of the wall that we see today was built during the Ming Dynasty. By the time this wall was built, things had improved. The workers were treated better, and better tools made the task easier.

Much of the new wall was built in the same way as the first wall. However, the frame was now made of stone blocks or bricks rather than wood. It was left in place when the wall was finished.

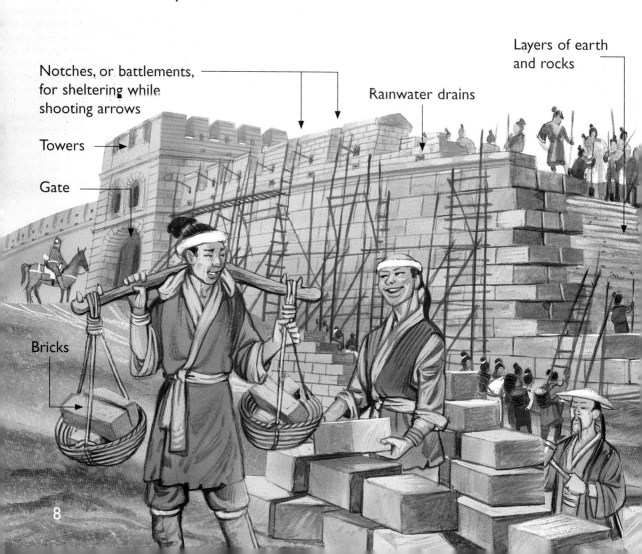

Notches, or battlements, for sheltering while shooting arrows

Towers

Gate

Rainwater drains

Layers of earth and rocks

Bricks

# Technology in 1600

The base of the wall was made with strong stone blocks. They were cut out of quarries and carried to the site.

Bricks were hardened in a special fiery oven called a *kiln*. These bricks were stronger than sun-baked bricks.

**quarry** a place where building stone is cut out of the ground

Strong stone blocks

The frame was filled with rocks, rubble, and earth. Layers were pounded down until they were solid.

# Getting Supplies

Today, trucks deliver supplies to building sites. When the Great Wall was built, donkeys carried in some food and supplies from other places. However, most of the building materials for the wall were gathered locally. It took a long time for donkeys to travel to the building site, and each donkey could carry only a small load. To prevent bandits from stealing the goods, guards were used.

material    something, such as wood or stone, that is used to make other things

This truck is delivering a huge load of bricks to a building site. A crane is used to help unload the supplies.

The first wall was made with dirt and rubble, or stone.

Bamboo grows throughout much of China. Workers tied bamboo poles together with rope to make frames and ladders.

Bamboo, reeds, or other plant materials were used to weave baskets.

11

# Tools for the Job

Tools make work easier. Today we have all sorts of tools to help with lifting, carrying, pushing, pulling, and cutting. They are mass produced in factories, which makes them cheaper to buy.

The people who worked on the Great Wall did not have all the tools we have today. Some tools had not been invented yet. Others were too expensive for most people.

The Chinese were some of the first people to use wheelbarrows. When the Ming Wall was built, they used them to carry loads around the building site.

mass produce   to make many items of the same thing at once

Many modern tools are powered by electricity or fuel rather than human muscles.

The long handles on tools such as wheelbarrows make work easier. They are called *levers*. Try this experiment to see how levers work.

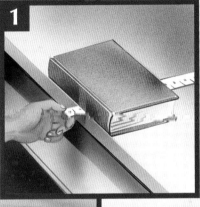

1. Rest a wooden yardstick on a table with about 1 inch sticking over the edge. Lay a heavy book on top of the stick so that it lines up with the table edge.

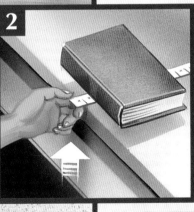

2. Carefully, lift the yardstick. How heavy does the book feel?

3. Repeat the experiment with about 12 inches of ruler between you and the book. How heavy does the book feel this time? Try different lengths. What do you notice?

# Lifting Loads

The Great Wall was tall. In some places, it was 25 feet high. That is about as high as a two-story house. The builders had to get their materials all the way to the top of the wall.

When the first wall was built, workers used ladders or tied full baskets to ropes and pulled them to the top. This was hard work. By the time the Ming Wall was built, they had simple machines called *pulleys* to make the job easier.

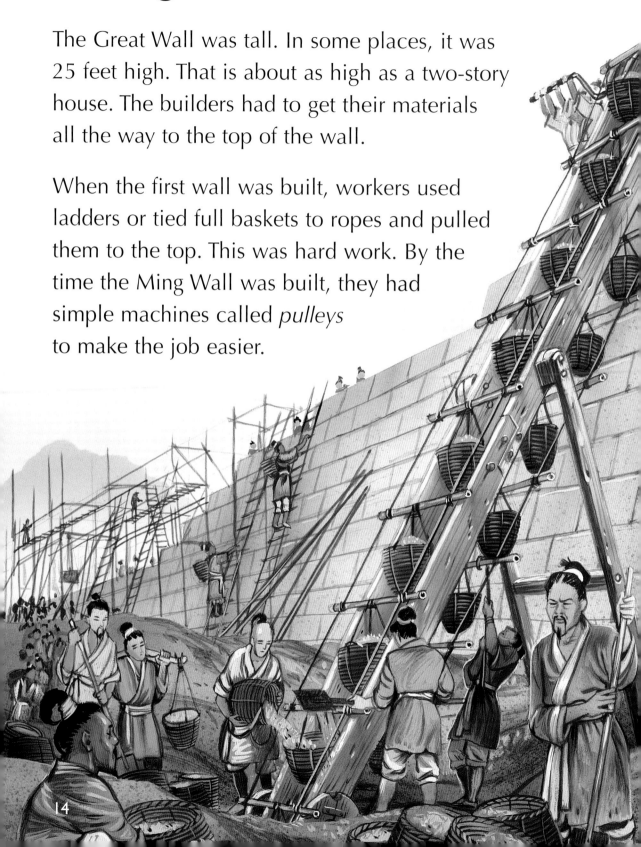

# Pulleys Help Pull

In this pulley system, a rope runs around a wheel. It lets the worker lift the weight by pulling from below. This is easier than pulling it from above.

A pulley system with two wheels makes lifting even easier. A worker has to be only half as strong to lift the load. However, it takes longer to lift it, because twice as much rope needs to be pulled.

The Ming Wall workers used ropes and pulleys to move materials across valleys and rivers. Full baskets were pulled from one side to the other.

Cranes lift goods to the top of modern building sites. Inside a crane is a pulley system. Machines are used to operate the pulley.

# Great by Design

The Great Wall was designed to be a huge fort. The workers built many tall towers along the wall. The towers were often so close together that anyone attacking the wall could be seen from a tower.

Many of the towers were two stories high. Food and weapons were stored in them. There were also rooms for the guards and stables for the horses.

**design** to plan what something will be like before you make it

The Great Wall has about 25,000 towers altogether.

Guards shot arrows through the gaps along the top of the wall.

There were no telephones when the wall was built. Guards used smoke, fires, flags, and gunshots to pass messages quickly from one tower to the next.

# Designs That Worked

Dirt for construction was often dug up just beyond the outside edge of the wall. The digging created a deep moat, which made it even harder for attackers to get in.

The Ming Wall had built-in drains to prevent water from slowly breaking it down. Rain and melted snow ran into the drains and out of the spouts on the attackers' side.

# Gates and Passes

Guards, traders, and farmers often needed to get
from one side of the wall to the other. They went
through passes. A pass was a gate surrounded
by a huge tower. It was guarded by about
one hundred soldiers.

The gap for the gate had a curved top,
called an *arch*. Inside the arch were
heavy, wooden double doors.

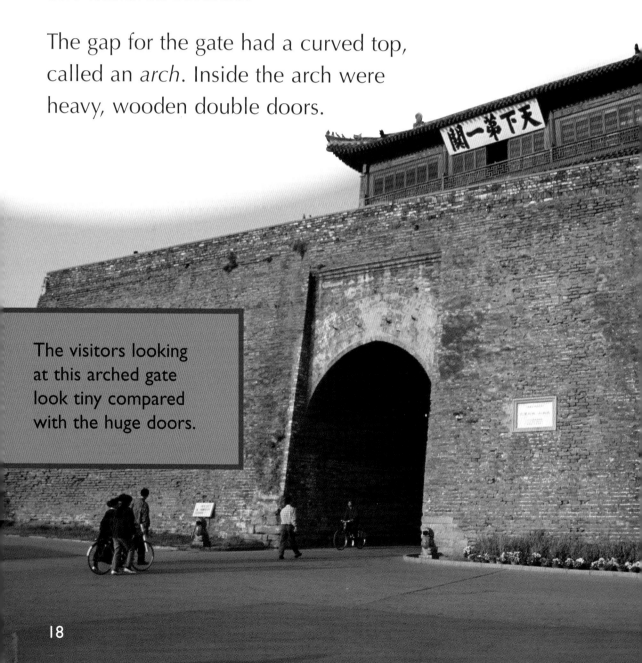

The visitors looking
at this arched gate
look tiny compared
with the huge doors.

Many of the windows and doors on the towers are arch shaped.

## Arches for Strength

Builders have used arches for thousands of years. The arch is a very strong shape. Its curved edge spreads the weight above it so that it does not fall down. About 1,400 years ago, Li Chun in China designed an arched bridge. It was stronger than other bridges and used less stone.

When the wall had to cross a stream, the workers built a water gate. This was a wall with big gaps in it for the water to flow through.

Nearly 1,900 years ago, the Romans took over England and built a wall a bit like the Great Wall. It was called Hadrian's Wall, and it had arched gates, too.

19

# Reaching the Top

The top of the wall was a busy place, even during times of peace. Guards used the top of the wall as a road. It allowed them to move quickly from one tower to another. They even rode horses and drove carts along it.

People got onto the wall by climbing stairs or ladders inside the towers and gates. Horses and carts used ramps to get to the top.

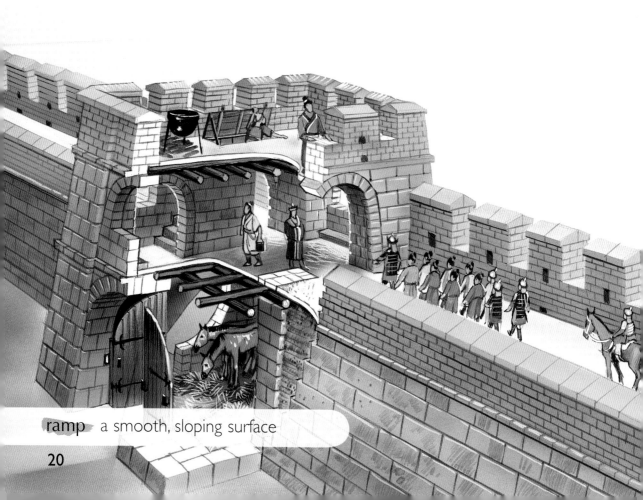

ramp    a smooth, sloping surface

Today, many visitors to China go to see the Great Wall. They often walk a little way along the top of it.

The Great Wall builders also used ramps. They would roll heavy rocks up a ramp to get them to the top of the tower.

# Modern Ramps

Today, we still use ramps in places where we cannot use stairs. Drivers use ramps to get around large parking garages.

People use ramps to get wheelchairs in and out of buildings.

Playground slides are ramps that we use just for fun.

# The Great Wall Today

No wall is tall enough to keep out modern planes
or missiles. Today, the Great Wall is no longer
used as a fort, but it does have other uses.
Archaeologists study it to learn about China's past.
Visitors travel from all over the world to see it.

Much of the wall is falling down.
Once again, Chinese workers
are rebuilding it. In some
places, they are using the
old methods.

archaeologist    a scientist who studies things
                 left by ancient societies

This huge kiln is full of new bricks for fixing the wall.

These modern workers are using stones on sticks to pound the earth. They want to fix the wall in the same way that it was built.

This picture of the Great Wall was taken from a satellite in space. Some people have said that the Great Wall can be seen from the Moon; however, this is not true.

# Find Out More!

1. What tools and machines do you use to make your life easier?

2. Do you think the people fixing the wall today should use old or new methods? Why?

To find out more about the ideas in *The Greatest Wall of All*, visit **www.researchit.org** on the web.

# Index

| | |
|---|---|
| arches | 18–19 |
| gates | 18–20 |
| levers | 13 |
| materials | 6–11, 14 |
| passes | 18 |
| pulleys | 14–15 |
| ramps | 20–21 |
| tools | 4, 7–8, 12–13 |
| towers | 7–8, 16–21 |